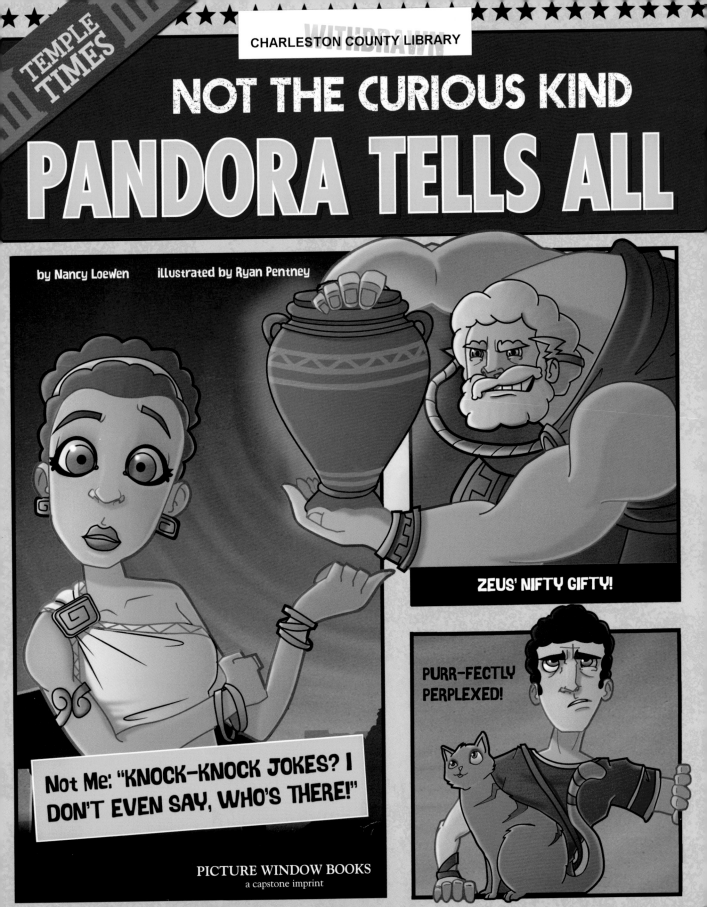

In Greek mythology Pandora was a woman created by the gods. She was given many gifts, including beauty, charm, and knowledge of the arts. But this lovely woman was no gift for humans—she was sent to Earth as a punishment.

Zeus, the king of the gods, was angry because Prometheus had stolen fire from the gods and given it to humans. He chained Prometheus to a rock. Every day a giant bird came and pecked at Prometheus' liver.

But Zeus' anger wasn't finished. He ordered a woman to be made out of clay and then given as a bride to Epimetheus, Prometheus' brother. As a wedding present, Zeus gave the couple a vase but told them they must never open it. Just as Zeus had planned, Pandora was overtaken by curiosity. She opened the vase—and out flew all of the sorrows that trouble humankind today: disease, hunger, old age, and war. By the time Pandora replaced the lid, Hope was all that was left.

That's the classic version of the story.
But how would Pandora tell it?

I didn't do it!

It wasn't ME who opened that vase against Zeus' orders and let out all those awful troubles. People say my curiosity got the best of me. Please! I'm not the curious type at all. When someone tells a knock-knock joke, I don't even say, "Who's there."

No, I didn't do it.

But I know who did.

Let's start at the beginning. MY beginning. My very first memory was of being presented to the gods. Hephaestus, my creator, led me by the hand. "Ta-da!" he said. "She's my best work yet!"

"She's beautiful," Aphrodite agreed. "But she needs a few finishing touches." She sprinkled glitter on me. Instantly my hair became as shiny as a jewel, my skin as smooth as a pearl.

Athena draped me in fine cloths. "But looks aren't everything," she said. Then she touched my forehead, and my mind was suddenly whirling with images of fantastic needlework and paintings. And somehow I knew exactly how to create them.

Hermes simply winked at me. I winked back. He had given me the gifts of charm and cleverness.

Then the Graces came fluttering in, adding earrings, bracelets, and a necklace. They dressed my head with a crown of spring flowers.

Finally Zeus himself nodded his approval. "Epimetheus will never be able to resist her. She'll bring those humans down a peg or two!"

The next thing I knew, I was standing with Hermes in front of a house. "Special delivery from Zeus!" Hermes announced.

Epimetheus opened the door, a cat in his arms. His jaw dropped when he saw me. I think he might have drooled a little.

Hermes nudged me, and my instincts kicked in. "Hello, I'm Pandora," I said, batting my eyelashes. "What a sweet cat!"

"Thanks," Epimetheus said shyly. "His name is Cuddles."

Hermes looked at his watch. "Oops! Gotta go. You kids have fun."

You can guess what happened next. Epimetheus and I fell in love and got married. Life was good—except for that cat. Oh, I loved Cuddles dearly, but he was always getting into trouble.

He batted my bracelets.

He "helped" me cook.

He used his tail
as a paintbrush.

He got stuck in chests,
trapped in closets ...

and tangled in
my knitting.

One day, soon after we were married, we received a wedding gift from Zeus. It was a large lovely vase with a lid.

"Maybe Zeus is finally getting over his grudge about my brother letting people have fire," Epimetheus said.

"I'm not so sure," I said, after reading Zeus' note. "He says we're not supposed to open the vase, ever. Do you think he's up to something?"

Epimetheus wasn't worried. "I can resist the temptation to open the vase," he said. "Can you?"

"Oh, please," I said. "The whole world is new to me! Why would I care about a silly old vase?"

But while we could resist the temptation of opening the vase, Cuddles was after it every chance he got.

I wanted to put the vase up in the attic, but Epimetheus decided that we should keep it in the living room. He liked showing off the vase to guests. "It was a wedding gift from Zeus!" he'd say as they oohed and aahed.

To me, he'd add, "I'll bet it drives Zeus crazy to see that we're not falling for his tricks!"

"Just don't blame me if Cuddles breaks it someday," I'd tell him.

One Saturday morning I woke up early. I thought I'd surprise my husband by cleaning the house before he got up.

I polished and swept my way through every room.

Finally I'd cleaned everything, except the shelf holding our special vase.

Usually I locked Cuddles in his crate before I cleaned the living room. But I found him curled up with Epimetheus, sleeping so peacefully you'd never guess what a troublemaker that cat was.

I let the sleeping cat lie.

Ever so carefully I placed the vase on the floor. And ever so quickly, I polished the shelf. I was just turning around when—

OH! The noise was deafening–like a million smoke alarms going off! An icy wind whipped through the house, shattering lamps and splintering chairs. Dark shadows flew at my head like vicious birds. I cried, knowing that nothing in the world would ever be the same.

And there was poor Cuddles, crouching in a corner, scared to death by what he'd done.

I groped around for the lid. Before I slammed it back onto the vase, I caught a glimpse of something glowing inside, like a tiny little sun. I knew that all was not lost. Inside the vase was Hope.

Just then the door exploded! The shadows flew out of our home and blackened the morning sky.

Epimetheus dashed into the room. "Pandora! Cuddles! Are you OK?"

I could have said "I told you so" to my husband, but I didn't. I was just so glad we were all safe.

So you see? It wasn't *my* curiosity that changed the world. It was my *cat's* curiosity!

Not that Cuddles is curious anymore. No more chests, closets, or vases for him! These days he sticks to laps.

Critical Thinking Using the Common Core ★ ★ ★ ★ ★ ★ ★

This version of the classic Greek myth is told by Pandora, from her point of view. If Epimetheus told the story, what details might he tell differently? What if Cuddles told the story from his point of view? (Integration of Knowledge and Ideas)

Pandora blamed Cuddles for opening the vase. But both she and Epimetheus made mistakes that led to the accident. Describe those mistakes. Do you think Pandora should have accepted more responsibility for what happened? Why or why not? Give examples to support your answer. (Craft and Structure)

Prometheus was the one who stole fire from the gods and gave it to humans. Zeus punished him, but he also punished humans. Explain the steps Zeus took to punish humankind. (Key Ideas and Details)

Describe the gifts Pandora received from the gods when she was created. How were these gifts important to Zeus' plan for punishing humans? (Integration of Knowledge and Ideas)

Glossary ★ ★ ★ ★ ★ ★ ★ ★ ★ ★ ★ ★ ★ ★ ★ ★ ★ ★ ★

mythology—old or ancient stories told again and again that help connect people with their past

needlework—crafts such as sewing, embroidery, or knitting

point of view—a way of looking at something

temptation—something that a person wants but shouldn't have

version—an account of something from a certain point of view

Read More

Kimmel, Eric A. *The McElderry Book of Greek Myths.* New York: M.K. McElderry Books, 2008.

McMullan, Kate. *Keep a Lid on It, Pandora!* Myth-o-Mania. Mankato, Minn.: Stone Arch Books, 2012.

Meister, Cari. *Pandora's Vase: A Retelling.* Mankato, Minn.: Picture Window Books, 2012.

Townsend, Michael. *Michael Townsend's Amazing Greek Myths of Wonder and Blunders.* New York: Dial Books for Young Readers, 2010.

Internet Sites

FactHound offers a safe, fun way to find Internet sites related to this book. All of the sites on FactHound have been researched by our staff.

Here's all you do:

Visit *www.facthound.com*

Type in this code: 9781479521814

 **Super-cool stuff!** Check out projects, games and lots more at **www.capstonekids.com**

Thanks to our advisers for their expertise, research, and advice:

Susan C. Shelmerdine, PhD, Professor of Classical Studies
University of North Carolina, Greensboro

Terry Flaherty, PhD, Professor of English
Minnesota State University, Mankato

Editor: Jill Kalz
Designer: Lori Bye
Art Director: Nathan Gassman
Production Specialist: Danielle Ceminsky
The illustrations in this book were created digitally.

Picture Window Books are published by Capstone,
1710 Roe Crest Drive, North Mankato, Minnesota 56003
www.capstonepub.com

Library of Congress Cataloging-in-Publication Data
Loewen, Nancy, 1964–
  Pandora tells all : not the curious kind / by Nancy Loewen; illustrated by Ryan Pentney.
    pages cm.—(Nonfiction picture books. The other side of the myth.)
  Summary: "Introduces the concept of point of view through Pandora's retelling of the
classic Greek myth 'Pandora's Vase'"—Provided by publisher.
  ISBN 978-1-4795-2181-4 (library binding)
  ISBN 978-1-4795-2956-8 (paper over board)
  ISBN 978-1-4795-2938-4 (paperback)
  ISBN 978-1-4795-3317-6 (eBook PDF)
1. Pandora (Greek mythology)—Juvenile literature. I. Pentney, Ryan, illustrator. II. Title.
  BL820.P23L64 2014
  398.20938'02—dc23   2013032211

photo credit: Hugo-Gunn Photography

About the Author

Nancy Loewen writes fiction and nonfiction for
children and young adults. Recent awards include:
2013 Oppenheim Toy Portfolio Best Book Award
(*Baby Wants Mama*); 2012 Minnesota Book Awards
finalist (*The LAST Day of Kindergarten*); and 2010
AEP Distinguished Achievement Award (Writer's
Toolbox series). She's also received awards from
the American Library Association, the New York
Public Library, and the Society of School Librarians
International. Nancy holds an MFA in creative
writing from Hamline University. She lives in the
Twin Cities area of Minneapolis – St. Paul.

Look for all the books in the series:

CYCLOPS TELLS ALL: THE WAY EYE SEE IT
MEDEA TELLS ALL: A MAD, MAGICAL LOVE
MEDUSA TELLS ALL: BEAUTY MISSING, HAIR HISSING
PANDORA TELLS ALL: NOT THE CURIOUS KIND

Printed in the United States of America in Brainerd, Minnesota.
092013   007770BANGS14